JE - - '19

Careers in Personal Space Travel

Martin Gitlin

Published in the United States of America by
Cherry Lake Publishing, Ann Arbor, Michigan
www.cherrylakepublishing.com

Reading Adviser: Marla Conn, MS, Ed., Literacy specialist, Read-Ability, Inc.

Photo Credits: Cover, Ase; page 4 (left), eHrach; Page 4 (right), Riksa Prayogi; page 6, FotograFFF; page 8, NASA Stock Images; page 10, Castleski; page 12, NASA Stock Images; Page 14, NikoNomad; page 16, Neo Edmund; page 18, FrameStockFootages; page 20, 3Dsculptor; page 22, Vadim Sadovski; page 24, colin13362; page 26, stockphoto mania; page 28, Money Business Images. Source: Shutterstock.

Library of Congress Cataloging-in-Publication Data

CIP data has been filed and is available at catalog.loc.gov.

Printed in the United States of America.

Table of Contents

Hello, Emerging Tech Careers!

In the past ...
Groundbreaking inventions made life easier in many ways.

In the present ...
New technologies are changing the world in mind-boggling ways.

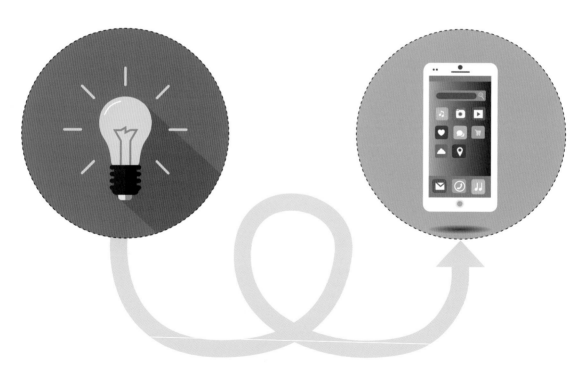

The future is yours to imagine!

WHAT COMES NEXT?

Who would have thought?

Alexander Graham Bell invented the first telephone in 1876.
In 1879, Thomas Edison invented the first electric lightbulb.
The Wright brothers successfully flew the first airplane in 1903.
And don't forget Henry Ford! He invented a way to make cars
quicker and cheaper.

These brilliant inventors did things that people once thought
were impossible. To go from candles to electricity? From
horse-drawn carriages to automobiles and airplanes? Wow!

The sky's the limit!

Now technology is being used to do even more amazing things!
Take **personal space travel**, for instance. Forget going to
the beach! One day you may be able to vacation on Mars or take
a sightseeing trip to the moon. Private companies like SpaceX
are already making the world say "wow!" with impressive
commercial rocket launches.

This book explores the people and professions behind personal
space travel. The idea that businesses and even individuals might
one day blast off into space is adding an exciting new twist to
careers like astronaut and aerospace engineer.

Read on to explore exciting possibilities for your future!

Aerospace Engineer

It is February 6, 2018. The rocket sits on the launchpad at the Kennedy Space Center in Florida. The countdown begins. "10, 9, 8..." But wait! This isn't a NASA rocket! It is the Falcon Heavy — the heaviest rocket ever built (so far). It was built by a private company called SpaceX. It has a red convertible Tesla on board, and it's about to make history.

An engineer applies math and science to solve real-life problems. Aerospace engineers design, build, and test aircraft and spacecraft. Engineers are critical to the success or failure of any personal space travel project.

Aerospace engineers fall into two categories. Some create and test craft that remain in Earth's atmosphere, such as the jet airplane. They are called aeronautical engineers. Others focus on craft that zoom into space. They are known as astronautical engineers.

There is a huge difference between the two. Those who work on rockets, missiles, and other spacecraft solve different kinds of problems. That is because the atmosphere in space is unlike Earth's atmosphere.

One example is the lack of airflow in space. Jet engines require the air in our atmosphere in order to function. Jet engines work well within Earth's atmosphere. But they could never

Imagine It!

- → Find a photo online that shows a rocket ship on a launchpad about to lift off.

- → Get a large sketch pad and a variety of colored pencils.

- → Draw what you see. Make it as detailed as possible.

Dig Deeper!

- ✓ The most famous space mission was *Apollo 11*. That American mission in 1969 sent astronauts to the moon for the first time. Read about it in *Moonshot: The Flight of Apollo 11* by Brian Floca (New York: Atheneum, 2009).

- ✓ Or read about the history of flight: *Flight* (A DK Eyewitness Book) by Andrew Nahum (New York: DK Publishing, 2011).

Curiosity is a car-sized rover designed to explore Mars as part
of NASA's Mars Science Laboratory mission.

work in a spaceship. Astronautical engineers must design spaceships that run on liquid oxygen and **propellant**.

Any spaceship transporting humans to other planets or on journeys around the universe must be safe and sound. Engineers who design them must first learn all about aerodynamics. That is the study of the interaction between air and moving objects such as rockets.

Manned missions into space require life-support systems. These provide air, food, water, temperature control, and human waste handling. Astronautical engineers will need to learn about all those concepts. They must gain a knowledge of physics and math.

They must also become familiar with materials science. Understanding alloys, polymers, and other high-tech building materials is crucial. Armed with this information, engineers can predict the success or failure of spacecraft designs before the building process begins.

Future Aerospace Engineer

High school students interested in this field should take classes in chemistry and physics. Also important are math courses such as algebra, trigonometry, and calculus. A college degree is required. Among the college subjects that train aerospace engineers are **propulsion** and mechanical engineering.

Astronaut

"Blast off!" Those two words are music to the ears of anyone interested in space travel. And the business of personal space travel has indeed blasted off. Astronauts are being trained to lead missions into outer space. Perhaps you can be one of those astronauts of the future!

It used to be that the nations of the world explored space independently. And until 1969, the United States and the former Soviet Union were in a space race. It ended that year when America became the first to land astronauts on the moon. Since then, countries have become partners in space exploration.

But a second space race has begun. Private companies are battling to be the first to transport passengers to Mars and beyond. These companies have strange names such as SpaceX, Virgin Galactic, and Blue Origin. They have built spaceships with futuristic names, like *Dream Chaser, Sundancer, Falcon 9,* and *Dragon*.

These companies have big plans. But they need astronauts. They are depending on facilities such as the NASTAR Center and SIRIUS Astronaut Training to prepare those who yearn to fly spaceships.

The training is not easy. Would-be astronauts must learn to overcome

Imagine It!

➡ Look up on the Internet all the private space travel companies. Compile a list of them.

➡ Read about each of those companies. Study what they are doing to reach their goals of transporting people into space.

➡ Decide which company you believe will be the most successful. Base your decision on your research.

Dig Deeper!

✓ Ask a parent or grandparent to join you online at http://easyscienceforkids.com/all-about-space-travel.

✓ Read about space travel history together. Then ask them about their memories of historic missions into space.

Dragon is the first commercial spacecraft in history to deliver cargo to the International Space Center in 2012 and return safely return to Earth.

space sickness. They must be able to handle sudden bursts of speed and being weightless. They must even deal with the possibility of hallucinations—seeing things that do not exist.

Training centers use testing grounds to teach students what to expect in space. A rotating room simulates varying degrees of **gravity**. A tilting device makes potential astronauts disoriented. A cylinder in a room with striped walls spins at a different speed than the floor on which the students stand. That induces **optical illusions** that can be common in space.

Such training can be hard and unpleasant. But it is realistic. It prepares astronaut hopefuls for the demands of their jobs. It is fun and exciting to dream of becoming an astronaut. Those who can handle the challenges of hurtling through space are on their way. They can make this fun and exciting career a reality.

Future Astronaut

Becoming an astronaut requires a lot of education and training. One must earn a college degree in math or one of many sciences. At least three years of professional experience or 1,000 hours of pilot-in-charge time on a jet aircraft is needed. A complete physical and astronaut training must also be completed.

Astronomer

Do you ever stare into the sky on a clear night? You see the moon and stars and distant planets. They are beautiful, shiny mysteries. You wonder what you cannot see. Is there life in outerspace? Some people become so fascinated by such mysteries that they become astronomers.

Space travel was born in the 1950s. But it was the science of **astronomy** that made it possible. Italian astronomer Galileo Galilei was the first to use a telescope to examine the **cosmos**. Space missions have just begun to explore what Galileo studied.

Astronomers research stars, planets, and other bodies that make up the universe. Personal space travel could never be possible without their work. They use information to create theories about the universe. They examine how it works and how its **celestial** bodies were formed.

Some astronomers seek to learn how the universe itself came into being. Others study specific bodies such as **galaxies**, planets, stars, and the sun.

Such knowledge is critical to the personal space travel industry. Companies that plan to escort humans into space must understand what astronauts and spaceships can expect along the way.

Imagine It!

→ The five planets visible without a telescope are Mercury, Venus, Mars, Jupiter, and Saturn. Use the Internet to find where they are in the sky.

→ Plot each of those planets on a sheet of paper.

→ Head outside on a clear night and see if you can find all five planets.

Dig Deeper!

✓ Go to this website and learn as much as you can about famous astronomers: http://easyscienceforkids.com/famous-astronomers-video-for-kids/.

✓ Think about which astronomer is your favorite. Decide why you picked that one.

Astronomers use data gathered by satellites to learn more about outer space.

One example is future vacations that might be spent on Mars. Astronomers and other scientists study that planet. They learn how people can live on its atmosphere. That information will be passed along to space travel companies and passengers, so they can survive and thrive on Mars.

Astronomers are often defined by the tools they use to study space. Optical astronomers use telescopes. They learn through observation of objects. Radio astronomers utilize radio telescopes instead. They study unseen radio waves given off by celestial bodies.

Not all astronomers examine information received on Earth. Some gather data from **probes** and **satellites** in outer space to study the universe.

Astronomers have a tougher job than other scientists. Astronomers study stars, planets, and other objects that are millions of miles away. That makes it harder to draw conclusions. But their work is critical to the future of personal space travel.

Future Astronomer

Astronomers require a high level of education. Those seeking a career in this field generally need a **PhD** in astronomy. One must pass complex math classes such as statistics, calculus, and linear algebra to succeed. Advanced studies in a specific field, such as planetary astronomy, is also required.

Atmospheric Scientist

What is the weather like outside? That is an easy question to answer. You just go out and you know. But what is the weather like way outside? Like millions of miles into space? That is what atmospheric scientists learn. Their work helps those planning space missions know what to expect along the way.

Many weather forecasters are seen on the television news. They predict conditions on Earth. They let the viewer know if it is going to be hot or cold, rainy or snowy, or dry. Those who study the weather are called meteorologists.

But not all meteorologists focus on the weather on Earth. Some are space scientists. They gather information with the help of satellite images, weather balloons, and radar systems. Some predict the weather and other events in the atmosphere. Others look at the history of weather patterns in various parts of the solar system. Still others seek out new ways to collect data and make predictions.

Many different fields fall under the category of atmospheric scientist. Their work can be applied to Earth and beyond. Among them is atmospheric chemistry, which examines the atmosphere on other planets. Another is climatology, which is the study of Earth's weather conditions and patterns over periods of time.

Imagine It!

➡ Learn all about the temperatures and atmospheres on the planets Venus and Mars.

➡ Decide which planet would best handle a new human civilization.

➡ Discuss your decision with your science teacher at school or any scientist you know. Find out if their conclusions match yours.

Dig Deeper!

✔ Click on the following space weather website for kids: www.spaceweather center.org/index.html.

✔ Read all about space weather. Decide what is the most fascinating fact you found on the website.

All aboard for outerspace!

Atmospheric scientists who might work in space travel will use their knowledge of weather and climate to study conditions in space. They analyze information to create short-term and long-term forecasts outside the atmosphere on Earth.

Their work will gain importance when personal space travel companies begin transporting passengers. Trip planners will need to know what weather and atmospheric conditions will be awaiting the astronauts and passengers. They will need to know what they can expect in outer space and when they arrive at their destinations.

Such information can be used to schedule space flights. It can be used to make certain the spacecraft is equipped to handle any difficult weather or atmospheric conditions. It can even be used to make sure passengers are equipped to deal with whatever atmospheric scientists predict will be coming their way.

Future Atmospheric Scientist

College students seeking degrees in atmospheric science take classes in meteorology, math, physics, and computer programming. One can begin a career in this field with just a bachelor's degree. But the study of weather, climate, and atmosphere in space requires much work and dedication.

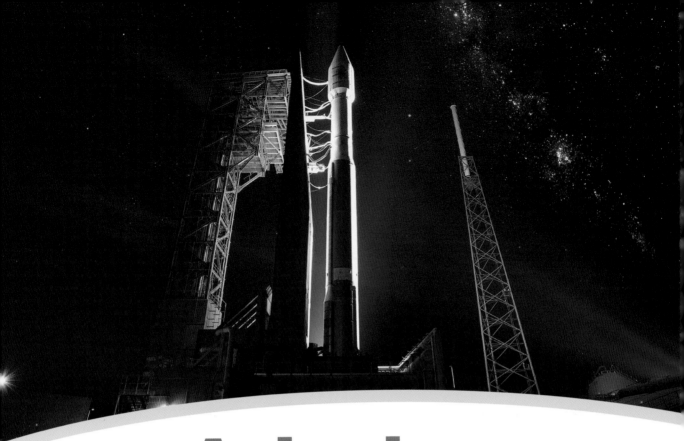

Avionics Technician

A mission to Mars is set for tomorrow. The rocket is on the launchpad. But testing shows an **electronics** problem. It must be fixed fast! Your company cannot cancel now. So they call you. You are an avionics technician. You rush to the scene and make the repair. You have saved the mission!

The equipment on spacecraft is complex. Those who repair it must be trained not just in electronics. They must learn all about the specific equipment on board. They have to know how to install, maintain, and fix everything. Their job is critical, especially if something goes wrong.

Avionics technicians perform a wide range of duties They schedule and perform regular **maintenance** on all spacecraft electronics. They also make urgent repairs.

They work with many different types of equipment. Included are navigation aids, radio communication devices, and radar systems. They must study and record flight test data for any signs of a problem. They have to make sure there is no threat to the safety of the spacecraft or anyone in it.

An avionics technician requires the skill to detect problems. The job requires an ability to assemble parts like electronic controls and to install

Imagine It!

→ Research the differences between the electronic equipment on an airplane and on a spacecraft.

→ Print out your information and use it to make a chart comparing the differences between airplanes and spacecraft.

Dig Deeper!

✓ Speak with a parent or teacher about building your own spacecraft. See if they will help you.

✓ Check out this website and follow its instructions: https://spaceplace.nasa.gov/build-a-spacecraft/en.

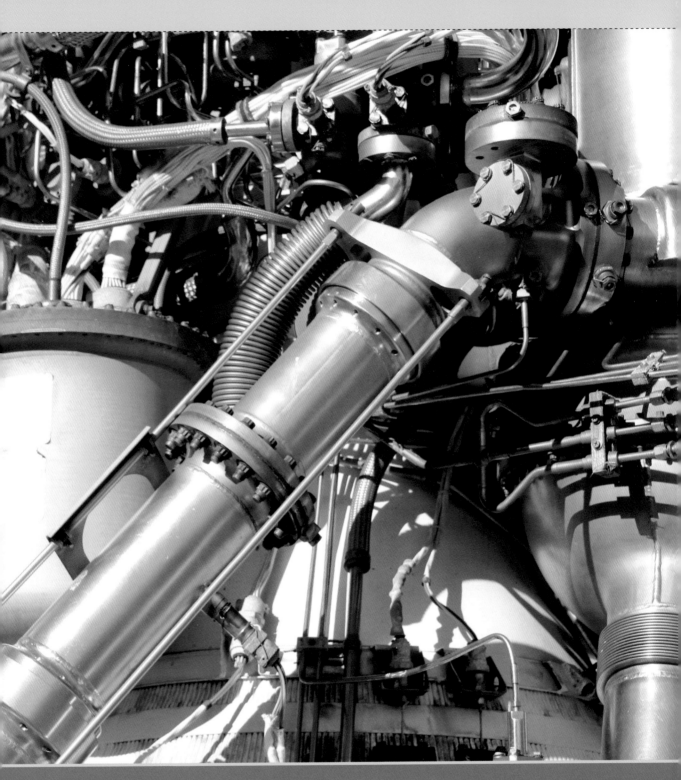

Avionics technicians must keep complex rocket engines in perfect working order.

new and replacement parts such as instrument panels. They must also be familiar with digital technology. That allows them to maintain computer systems used by the electronic instruments on board the spacecraft.

This job is critical to the success of a personal space travel operation. Avionics technicians are responsible for the instruments and equipment used to launch, track, position, and evaluate spacecraft.

That means communication skills are essential. Avionics technicians must confer with engineers about the details and results of equipment and flight testing. One must be a great listener and ask good questions about any potential problems. An avionics technician must think about the pros and cons of every possible solution to a problem. The job is too important to risk a mistake.

Future Avionics Technician

Personal space travel companies hire avionics technicians with a college degree in aerospace engineering. They prefer candidates with proven mechanical skills. Some might require previous experience in launch vehicle or spacecraft systems. Also needed are skills working with various hand tools and power tools.

Public Relations Specialist

Imagine you had the chance to tell the whole world how great it would be to take a spaceship to Mars. Or to explore the solar system. What methods would you use? Welcome to the worlds of public relations, media, and communications.

Personal space travel is a new industry. There is much to explain to the public. Personal space travel companies will want people to know that their crafts are safe. They will want people to believe that they will have the experience of a lifetime. They will want people to feel that their trip will be worth every penny they spend.

This is where the public relations staff comes in. They are hired to explain the science of space travel in easy terms. That way the public can understand. Running a personal space travel company is incredibly expensive. If they can't convince people to spend lots of money on space travel, they can't stay in business.

That's what public relations specialists do. They keep people informed about space discoveries and activities. They might update television news networks and online sites about company plans to build or test spacecraft. They might write news releases or blogs. Or they could arrange for school speakers to teach students about personal space travel.

Imagine It!

➔ Find out all you can about the plans of a personal space travel company to transport people to the planet Mars.

➔ Gather your family or a group of friends together.

➔ Now pretend you work in public relations for that company. Try to sell your family and friends on buying tickets for the trip. What would you tell them?

Dig Deeper!

✔ SpaceX is probably the best-known personal space travel company. Learning about SpaceX is a great start to learning about the future of personal space travel.

✔ Go to this website for kids and check out videos of SpaceX activities: http://thekidshouldseethis.com/tagged/spacex.

Sometimes public relations specialist share important news in TV interviews.

Media and communications jobs are part of public relations. One of those jobs is being a producer. Producers hire and work with film crews to create videos that educate the public about what their companies do.

Public relations specialists work with photographers to back up their words with images. Sometimes they use images taken by astronauts or special cameras in space. Other times they use images taken by Earth-bound photographers of the spacecraft and the people who make personal space travel a reality. They capture important moments in the progress of a project. Their work creates a visual timeline of a space mission from start to launch.

The science of space travel is hard to understand. Those in public relations and communications make it easier to understand. They try to make it fun and exciting. They seek to help the company sell its services to people. They hope to see those people aboard when their company is ready to escort folks into outer space.

Future Public Relations Specialist

A college degree in public relations would be helpful. Among the college courses one must take to earn that degree are media relations, marketing, advertising, and journalism. But learning the science and math involved in space travel would be wise, as well. It would also be helpful to land an internship with a personal space travel company to gain experience.

Can You Imagine?

Innovation always starts with an idea. This was true for Alexander Graham Bell, Thomas Edison, Henry Ford, and the Wright brothers. It is still true today as innovators imagine new forms of personal space travel. And it will still be true in the future when you begin your high-tech career. So ...

What is your big idea?

Think of a cool way to work in personal space travel. Write a story or draw a picture to share your idea with others.

Please do **NOT** write in this book if it doesn't belong to you.
Gather your own paper and art supplies and get creative with your ideas!

Glossary

astronomy (uh-STRAH-nuh-mee) the study of stars, planets, and space

celestial (suh-LES-chuhl) having to do with the sky

cosmos (KAHZ-mohs) the universe

electronics (ih-lek-TRAH-niks) machines powered by electricity

galaxies (GAL-uhk-seez) very large groups of stars and planets

gravity (GRAV-ih-tee) the force that pulls things toward the center of the earth and keeps them from floating away

innovations (in-uh-VAY-shuhnz) new ideas or inventions

maintenance (MAYN-tuh-nuhns) the process of checking and repairing something to keep it in good condition

optical illusions (AHP-tih-kuhl ih-LOO-zhuhnz) things that trick your eye by seeming to be what they are not

personal space travel (PUR-suh-nuhl SPAYS TRAV-uhl) spacecraft that support travel in outer space for individual or commercial use

PhD (PEE AYCH DEE) the highest college degree, awarded to a person who has done advanced research in a particular subject; also called a doctorate

probe (prōb) unmanned exploratory spacecrafts designed to transmit information about its environment

propellant (pruh-PEL-uhnt) a chemical or fuel that pushes something forward when it is burned

Index

About the Author

Martin Gitlin is a freelance author based in Cleveland. He has had more than 110 books published. He won more than 45 writing awards during his 11 years as a newspaper journalist, including first place for general excellence from the Associated Press. That organization selected him as one of the top four feature writers in Ohio in 2001.